UNSTOPPABLE
BUSINESS

TORREY HASH

DEDICATION

"To my beloved Kelly, who has always appreciated the wonder of robots, both mechanical and digital. It is through her fascination and support that I have delved deeper into the world of AI, and for that, I am forever grateful."

TABLE OF CONTENTS:

INTRODUCTION:

Building a successful business in today's economy is more important than ever before. With increased competition and rapidly changing market conditions, businesses must be agile and adaptable in order to survive and thrive.

A successful business provides not only financial stability for its owners and employees, but also contributes to the larger economy by creating jobs and generating revenue. Moreover, a successful business can help to address social and environmental challenges by offering innovative solutions and products.

In today's digital age, businesses must also be able to leverage technology to their advantage. This means adopting new tools and strategies such as AI and machine learning to optimize operations, improve customer experiences, and stay ahead of the competition.

Ultimately, building a successful business is about creating value for customers and society as a whole. By focusing on this goal and leveraging the latest technology, entrepreneurs can build thriving businesses that make a positive impact on the world.

AI, or artificial intelligence, has the potential to be a powerful tool for achieving business success in a number of ways.

Firstly, AI can help businesses to optimize operations and increase efficiency. Through automation and machine learning, AI can streamline processes, reduce errors, and improve productivity. This can help businesses to save time and money, and to focus on higher value tasks that require human expertise.

Secondly, AI can be used to improve customer experiences. By analyzing data and understanding customer preferences and behavior, businesses can personalize interactions and offer tailored recommendations. This can improve customer satisfaction, increase loyalty, and ultimately drive sales.

Thirdly, AI can help businesses to make more informed decisions. By analyzing vast amounts of data and identifying patterns and trends, AI can provide insights that humans might miss. This can help businesses to make better strategic decisions, anticipate market changes, and stay ahead of the competition.

Finally, AI can help businesses to innovate and develop new products and services. By leveraging machine learning and natural language processing, businesses can identify unmet needs and develop solutions that address these needs. This can help businesses to stay relevant and competitive in a rapidly changing market.

Overall, AI has the potential to be a powerful tool for achieving business success by improving efficiency, enhancing customer experiences, enabling better decision-making, and driving innovation. As such, businesses that invest in AI and leverage its capabilities are likely to have a significant competitive advantage over those that do not.

"Unstoppable Business: Leveraging AI for Success" is a comprehensive guide for entrepreneurs and business leaders looking to achieve long-term success in today's competitive economy. The book covers a range of topics and strategies, all centered around the use of AI as a powerful tool for business growth and innovation.

CHAPTER 1: DEFINING YOUR BUSINESS

Defining your business mission and goals is critical to the success of your business. It is important to have a clear understanding of what your business stands for and what you hope to achieve. This helps you to stay focused, make better decisions, and stay on track.

Here are some reasons why defining your business mission and goals is important:

Provides clarity: Defining your business mission and goals helps to provide clarity about what your business is all about. This clarity can help you to make better decisions about how to allocate resources, what products or services to offer, and how to market your business. Focuses your efforts: Once you have a clear mission and goals for your business, you can focus your efforts on achieving those goals. This helps to ensure that you are working towards something meaningful and important.

Guides decision-making: Having a clear mission and goals helps to guide decision-making within your business. You can use your mission and goals as a reference point when considering new opportunities or making changes to your business.

Sets expectations: Your mission and goals can also help to set expectations for your customers, employees, and stakeholders. They can understand what your business stands for and what you hope to achieve, which can help to build trust and loyalty.

Measures progress: Defining your mission and goals also helps you to measure your progress. You can track your performance against your goals and make adjustments as needed.

In summary, defining your business mission and goals is critical to the success of your business. It provides clarity, focus, guides decision-making, sets expectations, and helps you to measure progress. By taking the time to define your mission and goals, you are setting your business up for long-term success.

AI can be a powerful tool for identifying your target audience and market niche. With AI, businesses can analyze large amounts of data to identify patterns and trends that can help them better understand their customers and target market.

Here are some ways in which AI can be used to identify your target audience and market niche:

Data analysis: AI can be used to analyze large amounts of data to identify patterns and trends in customer behavior. This data can be used to identify common characteristics among your target audience, such as age, gender, location, and interests.

Predictive analytics: AI can also be used to make predictions about customer behavior based on past data. This can help businesses to better understand what their customers are looking for and how they can meet their needs.

Natural language processing: AI can be used to analyze customer feedback and reviews to better understand their needs and preferences. This can help businesses to improve their products or services to better meet the needs of their target audience.

Image recognition: AI can also be used to analyze images and videos to identify common themes and trends. This can be helpful for businesses that rely on visual content to reach their target audience.

Real-world examples of AI being used to identify target audiences and market niches include: Netflix: Netflix uses AI to analyze user behavior to make personalized recommendations for movies and TV shows. This has helped them to better understand their target audience and improve customer engagement.

Amazon: Amazon uses AI to analyze customer purchase history and browsing behavior to make personalized product recommendations. This has helped them to better understand their customers and improve their product offerings.

Coca-Cola: Coca-Cola used AI to analyze social media conversations to identify common themes and preferences among their target audience. This helped them to develop new product offerings that better met the needs of their customers.

In summary, AI can be a powerful tool for identifying your target audience and market niche. By analyzing large amounts of data, businesses can better understand their customers and develop products or services that meet their needs. Real-world examples from companies like Netflix, Amazon, and Coca-Cola demonstrate the effectiveness of using AI to identify target audiences and market niches.

There are many successful businesses that have used AI to define and refine their business strategy. Here are some examples:

Google: Google uses AI to power its search engine and advertising platform. AI is used to analyze user data to provide more relevant search results and personalized advertising. This has helped Google to improve the user experience and increase ad revenue.

Uber: Uber uses AI to optimize its pricing and dispatch algorithms. AI is used to analyze traffic patterns, demand, and driver availability to provide more efficient and cost-effective rides. This has helped Uber to improve its bottom line and provide better service to its customers.

Starbucks: Starbucks uses AI to optimize its store locations and menu offerings. AI is used to analyze customer data and sales patterns to identify the best locations for new stores and the most popular menu items. This has helped Starbucks to improve customer satisfaction and increase revenue.

IBM: IBM uses AI to optimize its business processes and product offerings. AI is used to analyze customer data and market trends to identify new business opportunities and improve existing products. This has helped IBM to stay ahead of its competitors and remain a leader in the tech industry.

Tesla: Tesla uses AI to optimize its self-driving technology and improve vehicle safety. AI is used to analyze sensor data and make real-time decisions about vehicle control and safety. This has helped Tesla to improve its brand image and provide a safer driving experience for its customers.

These are just a few examples of successful businesses that have used AI to define and refine their business strategy. By leveraging the power of AI, these companies have been able to improve their products and services, increase revenue, and stay ahead of their competitors.

CHAPTER 2: UNDERSTANDING YOUR CUSTOMERS

AI can help businesses understand their customers' needs and preferences in a variety of ways. Here are some examples:

Sentiment analysis: AI can analyze social media posts, customer reviews, and other online content to determine the sentiment behind them. This can help businesses understand how their customers feel about their products, services, and brand.

Predictive analytics: AI can use customer data to predict future behavior and preferences. This can help businesses anticipate what their customers will want and adjust their offerings accordingly.

Personalization: AI can use customer data to create personalized experiences, such as product recommendations or targeted marketing campaigns. This can help businesses improve customer satisfaction and loyalty.

Chatbots: AI-powered chatbots can interact with customers in real time and provide personalized assistance. This can help businesses improve customer service and support.

Voice assistants: AI-powered voice assistants, such as Amazon Alexa or Google Assistant, can help businesses understand customer preferences and behavior through voice commands and interactions.

By using AI to understand their customers' needs and preferences, businesses can improve their products and services, increase customer satisfaction and loyalty, and ultimately drive revenue growth.

Collecting and analyzing customer data is crucial for businesses to understand their customers' needs and preferences, as well as to make informed business decisions. Here are some reasons why collecting and analyzing customer data is important:

Customer insights: By collecting and analyzing customer data, businesses can gain insights into their customers' behavior, preferences, and needs. This information can help businesses improve their products and services, develop targeted marketing campaigns, and create personalized experiences for their customers.

Competitive advantage: By collecting and analyzing customer data, businesses can gain a competitive advantage over their competitors. By understanding their customers better than their competitors, businesses can create more effective marketing campaigns and offer more relevant products and services.

Data-driven decision-making: Collecting and analyzing customer data can help businesses make data-driven decisions. Instead of relying on guesswork or intuition, businesses can use customer data to make informed decisions about product development, marketing, and other aspects of their business.

Improved customer experience: By collecting and analyzing customer data, businesses can improve the customer experience. By understanding their customers' needs and preferences, businesses can create personalized experiences that meet their customers' expectations.

Revenue growth: Collecting and analyzing customer data can ultimately lead to revenue growth. By understanding their customers better, businesses can improve their products and services, increase customer loyalty, and ultimately drive more sales.

In summary, collecting and analyzing customer data is essential for businesses to understand their customers' needs and preferences, make informed decisions, gain a competitive advantage, and ultimately drive revenue growth.

Here are some examples of companies that have used AI to improve customer engagement and loyalty:

Starbucks: The coffee giant uses AI-powered customer engagement tools to personalize its mobile app experience for customers. The app provides personalized recommendations, order history, and promotions based on customer preferences and purchase history. This has helped Starbucks increase customer loyalty and engagement.

Sephora: The beauty retailer uses AI-powered chatbots to provide personalized beauty advice to customers. The chatbots can recommend products based on customer preferences and answer questions about ingredients and application. This has helped Sephora improve customer engagement and satisfaction.

Amazon: The e-commerce giant uses AI to provide personalized product recommendations to customers. By analyzing customer data, Amazon can recommend products that are relevant to each customer's interests and preferences. This has helped Amazon increase customer engagement and loyalty.

Domino's Pizza: The pizza chain uses AI-powered chatbots to take orders and answer customer questions. The chatbots can also track orders and provide updates on delivery times. This has helped Domino's improve customer satisfaction and loyalty.

Hilton Hotels: The hotel chain uses AI-powered chatbots to provide personalized recommendations and assistance to guests. The chatbots can recommend restaurants and local attractions based on customer preferences and answer questions about hotel amenities. This has helped Hilton improve customer satisfaction and loyalty.

Companies across industries are using AI to improve customer engagement and loyalty by providing personalized experiences, recommendations, and assistance. By leveraging AIpowered tools, businesses can increase customer satisfaction and ultimately drive revenue growth.

CHAPTER 3: DEVELOPING YOUR BRAND

Branding plays a crucial role in building a successful business for several reasons:

Differentiation: In a crowded marketplace, a strong brand helps a business stand out from the competition. A well-defined brand identity can help communicate a unique value proposition and differentiate a business from its competitors.

Trust: A strong brand can build trust with customers. When a brand consistently delivers on its promises and provides a positive customer experience, it can create loyal customers who become advocates for the brand.

Recognition: A well-established brand can be easily recognized by customers, even in a noisy marketplace. This can help a business increase its visibility and attract new customers.

Premium pricing: A strong brand can command premium pricing for products or services, as customers are often willing to pay more for a brand they trust and value.

To build a successful brand, businesses need to focus on developing a clear brand strategy that encompasses the company's values, vision, and mission. This involves defining the brand's target audience, developing a unique brand personality, and creating a visual identity that represents the brand's values and personality.

AI can also play a role in building a successful brand by providing valuable insights into customer preferences and behavior. By analyzing customer data, businesses can identify patterns and trends that can inform brand strategy and messaging. For example, AI-powered tools can help businesses identify which marketing messages are resonating with customers and which are not, allowing them to refine their brand messaging for maximum impact.

In summary, branding is a critical component of building a successful business, helping to differentiate a business from its competitors, build trust with customers, and command premium pricing. By developing a strong brand strategy and leveraging AI-powered tools, businesses can build a brand that resonates with customers and drives revenue growth.

AI can be a powerful tool in creating a strong and memorable brand by providing valuable insights into customer preferences and behavior. Here are some ways AI can help:

Brand personality: AI-powered tools can analyze customer data to help businesses identify the personality traits that customers associate with their brand. This can help businesses refine their brand personality and messaging to better resonate with their target audience.

Visual identity: AI can be used to create or refine a brand's visual identity. For example, AIpowered design tools can analyze existing visual elements (such as a logo or color scheme) to identify patterns and suggest improvements.

Messaging: AI can help businesses refine their brand messaging by analyzing customer data to identify which messages resonate most with their target audience. This can help businesses create more effective messaging that speaks directly to their customers' needs and preferences. Personalization: AI can be used to create personalized brand experiences for customers. For example, AI-powered chatbots can provide personalized recommendations and support based on each customer's individual preferences and behavior.

Brand monitoring: AI can help businesses monitor their brand's reputation and identify potential issues before they become major problems. For example, AI-powered social media monitoring tools can identify negative sentiment and alert businesses to potential issues in real-time.

Overall, AI can help businesses create a strong and memorable brand by providing valuable insights into customer preferences and behavior, enabling businesses to refine their brand strategy and messaging for maximum impact. By leveraging AI-powered tools, businesses can build a brand that resonates with customers and drives long-term success.

There are many examples of successful companies that have leveraged AI to develop and promote their brand. Here are a few:

Coca-Cola: Coca-Cola has used AI to create personalized packaging for its customers. The company used an AI-powered algorithm to generate millions of unique designs, each one tailored to a specific consumer based on their name, interests, and location.

Netflix: Netflix uses AI to analyze customer data and create personalized recommendations for its users. By using AI to understand customer preferences and behavior, Netflix can suggest new content that users are likely to enjoy, leading to increased engagement and customer loyalty.

Sephora: Sephora has used AI to create a personalized shopping experience for its customers. The company uses an AI-powered tool called the Virtual Artist to help customers try on makeup virtually, enabling them to see how different products will look before making a purchase. Airbnb: Airbnb uses AI to personalize its search results for each user. By analyzing user behavior and preferences, Airbnb can suggest listings that are most likely to appeal to each individual user, increasing the likelihood of a successful booking.

Amazon: Amazon uses AI to power its recommendation engine, suggesting products that customers are likely to be interested in based on their past behavior and purchase history. This personalized approach has helped Amazon become one of the most successful e-commerce companies in the world.

Overall, these companies demonstrate how AI can be used to create a more personalized and engaging brand experience for customers, leading to increased loyalty and revenue. By leveraging AI-powered tools, businesses can gain a deeper understanding of their customers and create more effective branding strategies that resonate with their target audience.

CHAPTER 4: BUILDING YOUR TEAM

Building a strong team is crucial for the success of any business. Here are some reasons why:

Diverse skill sets: When building a team, it's important to bring together people with diverse skill sets. This helps ensure that your business has the knowledge and expertise it needs to tackle any challenges that may arise.

Increased efficiency: A strong team is more efficient than a group of individuals working separately. When team members are able to collaborate and share their expertise, they can complete tasks more quickly and with greater accuracy.

Improved morale: When employees feel that they are part of a strong team, they are more likely to feel valued and motivated to perform at their best. This can lead to improved morale and job satisfaction, which in turn can help reduce turnover and increase productivity.

Better problem-solving: A strong team is better equipped to solve complex problems and make strategic decisions. By bringing together people with diverse backgrounds and perspectives, you can ensure that your business is able to find creative solutions to even the toughest challenges. Support for growth: As your business grows, you will need a strong team to support you. By building a team with the right mix of skills and experience, you can ensure that your business is well-positioned to take advantage of new opportunities and overcome any obstacles that may arise.

Overall, building a strong team is essential for the success of any business. It requires careful planning, effective communication, and a commitment to creating a positive and supportive work environment. By investing in your team, you can help ensure the long-term success and growth of your business.

AI can be a powerful tool for identifying and recruiting top talent for your business. Here are some ways AI can help:

Screening resumes: AI-powered recruiting software can screen resumes and identify candidates who meet the qualifications you are looking for. This can help save time and ensure that you are only considering candidates who are a good fit for the job.

Candidate matching: AI can use data analytics to match candidates with the skills and experience you are looking for to the job requirements. This can help you find the best candidates for the job more quickly and accurately.

Behavioral assessments: AI-powered behavioral assessments can help you identify candidates who are a good fit for your company culture. These assessments use data analytics to analyze a candidate's communication style, work style, and other factors that can impact their performance on the job.

Interview scheduling: AI-powered scheduling tools can help you streamline the interview process by automatically scheduling interviews with candidates and sending out reminders.

Performance analysis: AI can help you analyze candidate performance data to identify areas where they excel and areas where they need improvement. This can help you make more informed decisions when hiring and help you identify ways to help your new hires succeed.

By leveraging AI in your recruiting process, you can save time, reduce bias, and identify the best candidates for your business more quickly and accurately. This can help you build a strong team that is equipped to take your business to the next level.

Here are a few examples of companies that have used AI to improve their hiring and retention practices:

Unilever: Unilever uses AI to screen job candidates based on their resumes and online assessments. The company also uses AI-powered chatbots to answer candidates' questions and provide feedback on their applications. This has helped Unilever speed up the hiring process and identify high-potential candidates more quickly.

Hilton: Hilton uses AI-powered assessments to evaluate job candidates and identify those who are most likely to succeed in their roles. The assessments analyze a candidate's skills, personality, and work style to determine their fit with the company culture. Hilton has found that this has helped them improve their retention rates and reduce turnover.

IBM: IBM uses AI to help identify employees who are at risk of leaving the company. The AI system analyzes employee data, such as performance reviews and survey responses, to identify patterns that are associated with turnover. This allows IBM to take proactive steps to address potential issues and retain valuable employees.

Siemens: Siemens uses AI to analyze job descriptions and identify language that is biased or exclusionary. The company has found that this has helped them attract a more diverse pool of candidates and improve their hiring outcomes.

These are just a few examples of how companies are using AI to improve their hiring and retention practices. By leveraging AI tools and technologies, businesses can streamline their recruitment processes, reduce bias, and identify the best candidates for the job. This can help them build strong teams that are equipped to achieve their business goals.

CHAPTER 5: MANAGING YOUR FINANCES

Financial management is crucial for running a successful business. It involves tracking and analyzing the financial activities of a business to ensure that it is making smart financial decisions and staying on track to achieve its goals.

Here are some reasons why financial management is so important:

It helps you make informed decisions: Financial data provides critical insights into the financial health of your business. By monitoring financial metrics like cash flow, revenue, and expenses, you can make informed decisions about how to allocate resources and invest in growth opportunities.

It enables you to plan for the future: Financial planning is an essential part of financial management. By creating budgets, forecasting future revenues and expenses, and setting financial goals, you can ensure that your business is on track to meet its long-term objectives.

It helps you manage risk: Financial management involves identifying and managing risks that could impact your business's financial stability. This could include managing cash flow, managing debt and credit, and creating contingency plans for unforeseen events.

It helps you measure performance: Financial data provides a clear picture of how your business is performing. By tracking financial metrics and analyzing financial data, you can measure the success of your business and make data-driven decisions to improve performance.

In short, financial management is a critical component of running a successful business. By staying on top of your finances and making smart financial decisions, you can ensure that your business is well-positioned for long-term success.

AI can be a powerful tool for tracking and managing finances in a business. Here are some ways that AI can help:

Automating financial tasks: AI can automate many of the repetitive and time-consuming financial tasks that businesses must perform, such as invoice processing, account reconciliation, and financial reporting. This can save time and reduce errors, freeing up staff to focus on more strategic tasks.

Forecasting and predictive analytics: AI can use historical financial data to create forecasts and predictive analytics that can help businesses make more accurate financial decisions. For example, AI can analyze sales data to predict future revenue, or analyze expense data to forecast future expenses.

Fraud detection: AI can help identify potential instances of fraud by analyzing financial data for anomalies or suspicious patterns. This can help businesses take action to prevent financial losses due to fraud.

Personalized financial advice: AI can provide personalized financial advice to businesses based on their financial data. For example, AI can suggest ways to optimize cash flow or reduce expenses based on an analysis of a business's financial data.

Real-time financial reporting: AI can provide real-time financial reporting that can help businesses stay on top of their finances and make decisions based on up-to-date information. AI can be a powerful tool for tracking and managing finances in a business. By automating repetitive tasks, providing predictive analytics, and offering personalized financial advice, AI can help businesses make better financial decisions and improve their financial performance.

Here are some examples of companies that have used AI to improve their financial management practices:

JP Morgan Chase: JP Morgan Chase has used AI to automate many of its financial tasks, such as analyzing customer data to identify fraudulent transactions and analyzing trading data to optimize trading strategies. The company has also used AI to create predictive models that help it forecast financial performance.

Intuit: Intuit, the maker of QuickBooks and TurboTax, has used AI to help small businesses manage their finances. For example, the company's QuickBooks software uses AI to automate tasks such as categorizing expenses and reconciling accounts.

BlackRock: BlackRock, the world's largest asset manager, has used AI to improve its investment strategies. The company uses AI to analyze market data and identify investment opportunities, as well as to manage risk in its investment portfolios.

PayPal: PayPal has used AI to improve its fraud detection capabilities. The company uses AI to analyze customer data and identify potential instances of fraud, such as unusual transactions or suspicious patterns.

American Express: American Express has used AI to help its small business customers manage their finances. The company's AI-powered platform, called "Business Class," provides personalized financial advice and insights based on a business's financial data.

These are just a few examples of companies that have used AI to improve their financial management practices. By leveraging AI to automate tasks, create predictive models, and analyze data, these companies have been able to improve their financial performance and better serve their customers.

CHAPTER 6: DEVELOPING YOUR PRODUCTS AND SERVICES

Developing high-quality products and services is crucial for the success of any business. Here are a few reasons why:

Customer satisfaction: Customers are more likely to be satisfied with products and services that meet their expectations in terms of quality. This can lead to increased customer loyalty and positive word-of-mouth referrals.

Competitive advantage: Businesses that offer high-quality products and services are often able to differentiate themselves from their competitors. This can give them a competitive advantage in the market and help them attract and retain customers.

Cost savings: Developing high-quality products and services can help businesses save money in the long run. For example, by reducing the need for rework or repairs, businesses can lower their costs and improve their profitability.

Reputation: Businesses with a reputation for producing high-quality products and services are more likely to be trusted by customers and partners. This can help them establish themselves as leaders in their industry and attract new opportunities.

To develop high-quality products and services, businesses need to prioritize research and development, invest in quality control and testing, and be willing to make changes based on customer feedback. By continuously improving the quality of their products and services, businesses can improve their reputation, attract new customers, and drive long-term success.

AI can help businesses optimize their product development process by providing data-driven insights and automating certain tasks. Here are a few ways AI can be used in product development:

Market research: AI can analyze large amounts of data to identify market trends, consumer preferences, and areas of opportunity. This information can be used to inform product development strategies and identify potential product features or improvements.

Design optimization: AI can be used to create and refine product designs based on user feedback, performance data, and other factors. This can help businesses create products that are more effective, efficient, and user-friendly.

Quality control: AI can be used to automate quality control processes, such as product testing and defect detection. This can help businesses identify and address product issues more quickly, reducing the risk of customer complaints or recalls.

Personalization: AI can be used to create personalized product recommendations based on customer data and preferences. This can help businesses increase customer satisfaction and sales by providing tailored products that meet specific needs.

By incorporating AI into their product development process, businesses can streamline operations, reduce costs, and create products that better meet the needs and preferences of their customers. This can help businesses gain a competitive advantage in the market and drive long-term success.

Here are a few examples of companies that have used AI to improve their product and service offerings:

Amazon: Amazon has integrated AI into several aspects of its business, including product recommendations, search results, and voice assistants. Through machine learning algorithms, Amazon is able to provide personalized product recommendations to its customers based on their browsing and purchase history. Additionally, the company's voice assistant, Alexa, uses natural language processing (NLP) to understand and respond to customer inquiries and commands.

Netflix: Netflix uses AI to personalize its content recommendations for users, using algorithms to analyze user viewing history and suggest new shows or movies based on their interests. The company also uses machine learning to optimize its streaming service, predicting network congestion and adjusting video quality accordingly.

Spotify: Spotify uses AI to personalize its music recommendations for users, analyzing listening habits and preferences to create personalized playlists and suggest new songs or artists. The company has also developed an AI-powered tool called "Spotify for Artists," which helps musicians and labels better understand their audience and optimize their marketing strategies.

Tesla: Tesla uses AI to improve its self-driving technology, which is integrated into its electric vehicles. The company's Autopilot system uses computer vision and machine learning to detect and respond to road conditions, other vehicles, and pedestrians.

By incorporating AI into their product and service offerings, these companies have been able to improve the customer experience, increase efficiency, and gain a competitive advantage in their respective markets.

Reasons AI keeps you ahead of the curve:

Improving Efficiency and Productivity

One of the primary advantages of AI is that it can improve efficiency and productivity. Through automation and machine learning, AI can streamline processes, reduce errors, and increase productivity. This can help businesses save time and money, and allow employees to focus on higher-value tasks that require human expertise.

For example, chatbots and virtual assistants can be used to automate customer service interactions, freeing up customer service representatives to handle more complex issues. Similarly, AI-powered scheduling tools can optimize employee schedules, reducing the time and effort required to create schedules manually.

Enhancing Customer Experiences

AI can also be used to enhance customer experiences. By analyzing data and understanding customer preferences and behavior, businesses can personalize interactions and offer tailored recommendations. This can improve customer satisfaction, increase loyalty, and ultimately drive sales.

For example, AI can be used to recommend products or services based on a customer's browsing and purchase history. Similarly, AI-powered chatbots can provide instant customer support, 24/7, improving the overall customer experience.

Enabling Better Decision-Making

AI can help businesses make better decisions by analyzing vast amounts of data and identifying patterns and trends that humans might miss. This can provide insights that can help businesses make better strategic decisions, anticipate market changes, and stay ahead of the competition. For example, AI can be used to analyze sales data and identify which products are most profitable, helping businesses to make better decisions about which products to promote or invest in. Similarly, AI can be used to analyze social media data to identify customer sentiment, helping businesses to adjust their messaging or marketing strategies accordingly.

Driving Innovation

AI can also help businesses to drive innovation by enabling them to develop new products and services. By leveraging machine learning and natural language processing, businesses can identify unmet needs and develop solutions that address these needs. This can help businesses stay relevant and competitive in a rapidly changing market.

For example, AI can be used to analyze customer feedback and identify areas where products or services could be improved. Similarly, AI can be used to develop new products or services based on customer needs that might not have been identified through traditional market research. Artificial intelligence (AI) has become a game-changing technology that is transforming businesses across industries. It is no longer just a buzzword or a futuristic concept, but a tangible tool that businesses can use to gain a competitive advantage. In today's world, where businesses face increasing competition and rapid technological advancements, leveraging AI can be the key to survival and growth.

CHAPTER 7: MARKETING AND PROMOTION

Effective marketing and promotion is essential for any business that wants to succeed in today's competitive market. It helps to create brand awareness, generate leads, and increase sales. Without effective marketing and promotion, even the best products and services may go unnoticed.

Marketing involves identifying and understanding your target audience, creating a unique value proposition, and communicating that proposition through various channels. Promotion, on the other hand, involves using those channels to reach your target audience and persuade them to take action.

In today's digital age, marketing and promotion have become even more important as consumers are bombarded with endless choices and advertisements. This is where AI can be a gamechanger. By leveraging the power of AI, businesses can create more targeted, personalized, and effective marketing and promotion strategies.

AI can help businesses to:

Analyze customer behavior and preferences: AI can analyze customer data to understand their behavior, preferences, and buying patterns. This information can be used to create more targeted and personalized marketing campaigns.

Predict consumer behavior: AI can use predictive analytics to anticipate consumer behavior, such as which products they are most likely to purchase, which channels they prefer, and when they are most likely to make a purchase.

Automate marketing tasks: AI-powered tools can automate repetitive marketing tasks, such as social media posting, email marketing, and customer segmentation. This allows marketers to focus on more strategic tasks.

Optimize advertising campaigns: AI can analyze advertising data to identify which campaigns are most effective and optimize ad placement, targeting, and messaging to increase ROI. Personalize content and offers: AI can analyze customer data to create personalized content and offers that are tailored to each customer's interests and preferences.

AI can help businesses to create more effective marketing and promotion strategies that are based on data and insights, rather than guesswork. By leveraging the power of AI, businesses can improve customer engagement, increase conversions, and ultimately grow their bottom line.

AI can help businesses develop and execute successful marketing campaigns in several ways.

One key benefit of AI is its ability to analyze vast amounts of data and provide insights into customer behavior, preferences, and trends. This information can be used to develop targeted marketing strategies that are more likely to resonate with potential customers.

AI-powered marketing tools can also help businesses personalize their marketing efforts by providing personalized recommendations and messages to individual customers based on their past behavior and preferences. This can improve customer engagement and loyalty, as well as increase the likelihood of conversions and sales.

Another way that AI can be used in marketing is through chatbots and virtual assistants. These tools can provide customers with personalized assistance and support around the clock, improving customer satisfaction and loyalty.

AI can be a powerful tool for businesses looking to develop and execute successful marketing campaigns. By providing insights into customer behavior and preferences, personalizing marketing efforts, and offering around-the-clock support, businesses can improve their marketing effectiveness and drive growth.

There are several companies that have successfully used AI to improve their marketing and promotional strategies. Here are a few examples:

Netflix: Netflix uses AI algorithms to recommend personalized content to its users based on their viewing history and preferences. This has helped to improve customer engagement and retention, as well as increase the likelihood of customers discovering new content.

Amazon: Amazon uses AI to personalize product recommendations for individual customers, based on their purchase history and browsing behavior. This has helped to increase sales and customer loyalty.

Sephora: Sephora has developed an AI-powered app that uses facial recognition technology to provide personalized makeup recommendations to customers based on their skin type and tone. This has improved customer satisfaction and loyalty, as well as increased sales.

Spotify: Spotify uses AI algorithms to recommend personalized playlists to its users based on their listening history and preferences. This has helped to improve customer engagement and retention, as well as increase the likelihood of customers discovering new music.

Coca-Cola: Coca-Cola has used AI to develop personalized marketing campaigns that target individual customers based on their preferences and behavior. This has helped to improve customer engagement and loyalty, as well as increase sales.

These companies demonstrate how AI can be used to personalize marketing efforts, improve customer engagement and loyalty, and increase sales.

In today's world, marketing companies are constantly searching for new ways to stay ahead of the competition and provide value to their clients. With the rise of artificial intelligence (AI), marketing companies now have a powerful tool that can help them optimize their strategies and deliver better results for their clients.

AI is changing the game for marketing companies in a number of ways. Here are just a few examples:

Improved Targeting

One of the most powerful ways that AI is changing the game for marketing companies is through improved targeting. AI-powered algorithms can analyze vast amounts of data, including customer behavior and demographics, to identify the most relevant audience for a given product or service. This means that marketing campaigns can be more precisely targeted to the right audience, leading to higher conversion rates and greater ROI.

Personalization

Another way that AI is changing the game for marketing companies is through personalization. By analyzing customer data and behavior, AI can help companies tailor their messaging and campaigns to the specific needs and preferences of individual customers. This can lead to greater engagement, loyalty, and sales. Chatbots and Customer Service

AI-powered chatbots are becoming increasingly popular in the world of customer service. These bots can answer common customer questions and provide assistance 24/7, freeing up human staff to focus on more complex issues. This can lead to faster response times, better customer satisfaction, and lower costs for marketing companies.

Predictive Analytics

AI-powered predictive analytics is another game-changer for marketing companies. By analyzing data from a wide range of sources, including social media and website traffic, predictive analytics can identify trends and patterns that can help companies anticipate customer behavior and preferences. This can help marketing companies stay ahead of the competition and develop more effective campaigns.

Content Creation and Optimization

AI is also changing the game for content creation and optimization. AI-powered tools can analyze existing content and provide insights into how it can be improved to better engage and convert customers. Additionally, AI-powered tools can assist with the creation of new content, such as product descriptions, blog posts, and social media updates.

AI is a game-changer for marketing companies. By leveraging the power of AI, marketing companies can provide greater value to their clients, deliver better results, and stay ahead of the competition. As AI technology continues to evolve, marketing companies will need to stay up-to-date with the latest tools and strategies to maintain their competitive edge.

CHAPTER 8: SCALING YOUR BUSINESS

Scaling a business can be both challenging and rewarding. On the one hand, scaling allows you to grow your customer base, increase revenue, and expand your market share. On the other hand, scaling a business requires a significant investment of time, money, and resources, and can be difficult to manage if not done properly.

One of the main challenges of scaling a business is maintaining the quality of your products or services while increasing production. This can be particularly difficult if your business is built around a personalized or handmade product. Another challenge is managing cash flow and ensuring that you have enough capital to finance your growth.

However, scaling a business also presents a number of opportunities. By scaling your business, you can take advantage of economies of scale, reduce costs, and increase profitability. You can also expand into new markets and reach new customers, which can help you build a stronger brand and increase customer loyalty.

To successfully scale a business, it's important to have a solid understanding of your target market and your competitive landscape. You should also have a clear understanding of your strengths and weaknesses and be able to identify areas where you can improve your operations and processes.

Additionally, it's important to have a strong team in place that can help you manage the challenges of scaling. This includes hiring the right people, providing them with the necessary resources and support, and ensuring that they have a clear understanding of your business goals and objectives.

Ultimately, scaling a business requires a combination of hard work, strategic planning, and effective execution. With the right approach and the right team in place, you can successfully grow your business and achieve long-term success.

AI can help businesses identify and pursue growth opportunities in several ways. For example, by analyzing customer data and market trends, AI can help businesses identify new market niches and customer segments. AI can also help businesses optimize their supply chain and production processes, allowing them to scale their operations more efficiently.

Another way AI can help businesses scale is by automating routine tasks and decision-making processes, freeing up human resources to focus on higher-level strategic tasks. This can help businesses become more agile and responsive to changing market conditions.

AI can also help businesses improve their customer engagement and retention, which is critical for long-term growth. By analyzing customer data, AI can help businesses personalize their marketing and customer service efforts, leading to higher levels of customer satisfaction and loyalty.

Overall, AI can be a powerful tool for businesses looking to scale their operations and pursue growth opportunities. By leveraging AI technologies and insights, businesses can make more informed decisions, optimize their processes, and improve their overall performance.

Here are a few examples of companies that have used AI to scale their businesses:

Amazon: As one of the world's largest online retailers, Amazon uses AI extensively to personalize the shopping experience for its customers. By analyzing customer data, Amazon can make product recommendations and offer personalized deals to encourage customers to buy more.

Netflix: As a streaming giant, Netflix relies heavily on AI to recommend movies and TV shows to its customers. By analyzing viewing patterns and other data, Netflix can suggest new content that users are likely to enjoy, keeping them engaged and subscribed.

Alibaba: As China's largest e-commerce company, Alibaba uses AI to help sellers optimize their listings and reach more customers. Alibaba's AI-powered product search algorithm helps buyers find what they're looking for more easily, while also helping sellers improve their product listings to increase sales.

Uber: As a leader in the ride-sharing industry, Uber uses AI to optimize its pricing and routes to increase efficiency and reduce wait times for customers. Uber's AI-powered algorithms also help the company identify areas where demand for rides is high, allowing them to deploy more drivers to those areas.

Spotify: As a music streaming service, Spotify uses AI to create personalized playlists for its users. By analyzing listening habits and other data, Spotify can create playlists that are tailored to each user's individual tastes, making the listening experience more enjoyable and engaging.

These companies demonstrate the power of AI when it comes to scaling a business. By leveraging the insights and capabilities provided by AI, they have been able to identify new opportunities for growth, increase efficiency and productivity, and provide better experiences for their customers.

Scaling a business is no easy feat. It requires careful planning, execution, and a deep understanding of market trends and customer needs. With the help of Artificial Intelligence (AI), however, businesses can achieve new levels of success by leveraging the insights and capabilities provided by AI to identify new opportunities for growth, increase efficiency and productivity, and provide better experiences for their customers.

One of the key advantages of AI is its ability to process and analyze large amounts of data quickly and accurately. By collecting data from a variety of sources, such as customer interactions, sales transactions, and social media, businesses can gain valuable insights into their customers' behavior and preferences. This information can then be used to develop more targeted marketing strategies, create personalized experiences for customers, and identify new areas for growth.

For example, an e-commerce company might use AI to analyze customer purchase data to identify patterns and trends in buying behavior. By understanding which products are selling well and to whom, the company can optimize its inventory, pricing, and marketing efforts to better meet customer needs and preferences. This can lead to increased sales and customer satisfaction.

AI can also be used to automate and streamline business processes, allowing companies to increase efficiency and productivity while reducing costs. For example, a manufacturing company might use AI to optimize its supply chain by predicting demand, identifying potential bottlenecks, and optimizing routes for delivery. By automating these processes, the company can save time and resources, and reduce the risk of errors.

In addition to improving efficiency and productivity, AI can also provide a better customer experience. By using AI-powered chatbots, businesses can provide 24/7 customer support, answer frequently asked questions, and help customers find the products and services they need. This can lead to higher customer satisfaction and loyalty.

Moreover, AI can help businesses to identify new areas for growth by uncovering unmet customer needs and preferences. For example, a hotel chain might use AI to analyze customer reviews and social media posts to understand what customers value most in their hotel experience. This information can then be used to develop new services and amenities that meet those needs and differentiate the business from its competitors.

AI has the potential to be a game-changer for businesses looking to scale and grow. By leveraging the insights and capabilities provided by AI, businesses can identify new opportunities for growth, increase efficiency and productivity, and provide better experiences for their customers. As such, companies that invest in AI are likely to have a significant competitive advantage over those that do not.

In addition to the methods already discussed, there are several other ways in which businesses can leverage AI to scale their operations and drive growth.

Predictive analytics: AI-powered predictive analytics can help businesses to forecast future trends, anticipate customer behavior, and identify potential areas of growth. By analyzing large amounts of data, AI algorithms can identify patterns and make predictions with a high degree of accuracy, helping businesses to make informed decisions about future investments and strategies.

Voice and image recognition: Voice and image recognition technologies are becoming increasingly sophisticated, allowing businesses to create more personalized and engaging experiences for their customers. For example, AI-powered chatbots can use natural language processing to understand customer queries and respond in real-time, while image recognition can be used to create personalized product recommendations based on a customer's browsing history. Supply chain optimization: AI can help businesses to optimize their supply chain, reducing costs and improving efficiency. For example, AI algorithms can analyze historical data to identify areas of waste or inefficiency in the supply chain, and suggest strategies to reduce costs and improve performance.

Fraud detection: AI can be used to detect and prevent fraud in real-time, helping businesses to protect themselves and their customers from financial losses. For example, AI algorithms can analyze transaction data to identify patterns of fraudulent behavior, and trigger alerts when suspicious activity is detected.

Social media analysis: AI-powered social media analysis tools can help businesses to monitor brand sentiment, track customer feedback, and identify opportunities for engagement. By analyzing large amounts of social media data in real-time, businesses can respond quickly to customer concerns and feedback, and tailor their marketing strategies to better target their audience.

In summary, AI has the potential to transform the way businesses operate and scale, providing new opportunities for growth, efficiency, and customer engagement. By leveraging the insights and capabilities provided by AI, businesses can stay ahead of the competition and thrive in today's rapidly changing economy.

Scaling a business can be a challenging task, as it involves increasing revenue while also maintaining the quality of products or services. Fortunately, advancements in technology have provided businesses with new tools to help them achieve this goal. One of the most powerful tools available today is AI, or artificial intelligence. By leveraging the insights and capabilities provided by AI, businesses have been able to identify new opportunities for growth, increase efficiency and productivity, and provide better experiences for their customers.

One of the primary ways that AI can help businesses to scale is by enabling them to make more informed decisions. By analyzing vast amounts of data and identifying patterns and trends, AI can provide insights that humans might miss. For example, AI can analyze customer behavior to identify patterns that indicate which products or services are in high demand. This information can then be used to inform product development and marketing strategies, enabling businesses to better target their audience and increase sales.

AI can also help businesses to streamline their operations, making them more efficient and productive. For example, AI-powered chatbots can be used to handle customer inquiries, freeing up human resources for more complex tasks. Similarly, AI can be used to automate routine tasks, such as data entry or invoicing, reducing the workload on employees and allowing them to focus on higher value tasks.

In addition to improving efficiency, AI can also help businesses to provide better experiences for their customers. By analyzing customer data and preferences, AI can enable businesses to personalize their interactions and provide tailored recommendations. This can improve customer satisfaction, increase loyalty, and ultimately drive sales.

Another way that AI can help businesses to scale is by enabling them to expand into new markets. By analyzing market data and identifying trends, AI can help businesses to identify new opportunities for growth and expansion. For example, AI can be used to analyze social media data to identify emerging trends and consumer preferences, which can inform product development and marketing strategies.

AI can help businesses to innovate and develop new products and services. By leveraging machine learning and natural language processing, businesses can identify unmet needs and develop solutions that address these needs. This can help businesses to stay relevant and competitive in a rapidly changing market.

Overall, AI has the potential to be a powerful tool for scaling businesses by enabling them to make more informed decisions, streamline operations, provide better customer experiences, expand into new markets, and drive innovation. As such, businesses that invest in AI and leverage its capabilities are likely to have a significant competitive advantage over those that do not.

CHAPTER 9: EXECUTIVE DECISIONS

Artificial Intelligence (AI) has revolutionized the way businesses operate by providing a wide range of tools and techniques for analyzing data, identifying patterns, and making predictions. One of the most significant advantages of AI is its ability to support executive decision-making by providing insights that might otherwise go unnoticed. In this chapter, we will explore how AI can help executives make sound business decisions through advanced research and analysis methods.

Predictive Analytics

Predictive analytics is a method that uses statistical algorithms and machine learning to analyze historical data and make predictions about future outcomes. With the help of predictive analytics, businesses can identify patterns and trends in customer behavior, sales performance, and other relevant factors that impact business success. By using predictive analytics, executives can anticipate changes in the market, identify new opportunities, and make informed decisions about resource allocation and investment.

Natural Language Processing (NLP)

Natural Language Processing (NLP) is a subfield of AI that focuses on the interaction between computers and human language. NLP techniques are used to analyze and understand text data, including social media posts, customer reviews, and other forms of unstructured data. By leveraging NLP, businesses can gain valuable insights into customer sentiment, preferences, and behavior. This information can be used to optimize marketing campaigns, improve customer experiences, and make more informed decisions about product development and innovation.

Decision Trees

Decision Trees are a type of algorithm that uses a tree-like structure to model decisions and their possible consequences. Decision Trees are particularly useful for executive decision-making as they provide a visual representation of complex decisions and their outcomes. By using Decision Trees, executives can identify the most effective course of action based on specific criteria and constraints. Decision Trees are particularly useful for complex decisions involving multiple factors and stakeholders.

Clustering

Clustering is a method used to group similar data points based on their characteristics. Clustering can be used to identify patterns and trends in customer behavior, sales performance, and other relevant factors. By using clustering, businesses can segment their customer base into groups based on shared characteristics such as demographics, interests, and behavior. This information can be used to tailor marketing campaigns, improve customer experiences, and optimize product development.

Simulation

Simulation is a method used to model real-world scenarios in a controlled environment. By using simulation, businesses can test different strategies and scenarios without the risk and expense of real-world implementation. This can be particularly useful for executive decision-making as it allows executives to evaluate the potential impact of different decisions before implementing them. AI can be a powerful tool for executive decision-making by providing insights that might otherwise go unnoticed. By using advanced research and analysis methods such as predictive analytics, NLP, Decision Trees, clustering, and simulation, executives can identify new opportunities for growth, increase efficiency and productivity, and provide better experiences for their customers. As such, businesses that invest in AI and leverage its capabilities are likely to have a significant competitive advantage over those that do not.

Artificial intelligence (AI) is rapidly changing the way businesses operate in a variety of industries. With its ability to process vast amounts of data and identify patterns and insights that may not be immediately apparent to humans, AI is now being used to assist business leaders in making sound executive decisions.

One of the most significant ways that AI is helping executives make better decisions is through predictive analytics. Predictive analytics uses machine learning algorithms to analyze past performance data, market trends, and other relevant data sets to forecast future outcomes. By providing accurate predictions about the future, executives can make informed decisions that reduce risk and increase the likelihood of success.

For example, an executive may use predictive analytics to analyze sales data from the previous year and identify which products or services are likely to see the most growth in the coming year. Armed with this information, they can make strategic decisions about how to allocate resources and invest in areas that are likely to yield the greatest returns.

AI is also being used to optimize decision-making processes. Through natural language processing and machine learning algorithms, AI can analyze and interpret unstructured data such as customer feedback, industry news, and social media conversations. This allows executives to make more informed decisions by taking into account a wider range of information sources. In addition, AI can be used to automate routine decision-making tasks. For example, an AIpowered chatbot can be programmed to answer frequently asked questions from customers, freeing up executive time to focus on more strategic decisions. This automation can also help to reduce errors and increase efficiency, leading to better overall business performance.

Another way that AI is helping executives make sound business decisions is through prescriptive analytics. Prescriptive analytics takes predictive analytics one step further by providing recommendations on what actions to take based on the predictions made. This can help executives to make more informed decisions that are grounded in data and evidence, rather than intuition or guesswork.

For example, an executive may use prescriptive analytics to identify the best marketing channels to use for a new product launch. Based on historical data and market trends, the AI system may recommend using social media and email marketing rather than traditional print advertising. By following this recommendation, the executive can increase the chances of success for the new product launch.

AI is revolutionizing the way that executives make business decisions. Through predictive analytics, optimization, automation, and prescriptive analytics, executives can leverage the power of AI to make more informed, data-driven decisions that reduce risk, increase efficiency, and drive growth. As the technology continues to advance, it is likely that AI will become an essential tool for any business looking to stay competitive in today's fast-paced and everchanging market.

As AI technology continues to advance and become more integrated into our daily lives, it's important to consider how we as individuals and businesses will use this technology and innovation.

For businesses, the potential benefits of using AI for decision-making are clear. By analyzing large amounts of data and identifying patterns and trends, AI can provide insights that humans might miss. This can help businesses to make better strategic decisions, anticipate market changes, and stay ahead of the competition.

However, it's also important to consider the potential downsides and ethical implications of using AI in decision-making. For example, AI algorithms may be biased based on the data they are trained on, leading to unfair or discriminatory decision-making. It's important for businesses to be aware of these risks and take steps to mitigate them.

As for individuals, the ways in which we use AI in decision-making will vary depending on the context. In our personal lives, we may use AI-powered devices and services to make decisions about what to buy, where to go, and how to manage our time. In professional contexts, we may use AI to help us make more informed decisions about investments, hiring, and other business decisions.

It's important for individuals to consider the potential benefits and risks of using AI in decision making, and to be aware of the limitations of the technology. While AI can provide valuable insights and improve decision-making, it's not a panacea for all problems and may have unintended consequences.

Overall, you must be thoughtful and deliberate in their use of AI for decision-making. By understanding the potential benefits and risks and taking a proactive approach to mitigating ethical concerns, we can ensure that AI is used to create a more equitable and just world

CHAPTER 10: LEVERAGING TECHNOLOGY FOR EFFICIENCY AND GROWTH

Technology has revolutionized the way businesses operate in today's world. It has enabled companies to operate more efficiently, cut costs, and scale faster. The use of technology has helped businesses automate tasks, access valuable data and insights, collaborate more effectively, and reduce time and resources required to complete projects. In this chapter, we will explore various ways in which technology, beyond AI, can help businesses scale more efficiently.

Automation: Automation refers to the use of technology to perform tasks that are repetitive and time-consuming. By automating certain processes, businesses can free up time and resources that can be redirected to more important tasks. Automation can help businesses scale by increasing efficiency, reducing human error, and improving productivity. For instance, businesses can automate their customer service through the use of chatbots, which can provide instant responses to customer queries and improve customer satisfaction.

Cloud Computing: Cloud computing allows businesses to store, access, and share data over the internet, rather than using physical hardware. This technology provides businesses with access to a scalable and flexible IT infrastructure, which can help them scale more efficiently. By using cloud-based tools and software, businesses can reduce costs, increase agility, and improve collaboration. For example, businesses can use cloud-based project management tools, such as Asana or Trello, to manage their projects and teams more effectively.

Project Management Tools: Project management tools enable businesses to plan, organize, and execute projects more efficiently. These tools can help businesses to manage resources, track progress, and communicate with team members effectively. By using project management tools, businesses can improve their project timelines, increase productivity, and scale more efficiently. For example, businesses can use project management tools such as Basecamp or Monday.com to collaborate and manage their projects.

Marketing Automation: Marketing automation refers to the use of technology to automate marketing tasks such as email campaigns, social media posts, and website updates. This technology can help businesses scale by allowing them to reach more customers with personalized messaging, without having to devote significant resources to these tasks. By using marketing automation, businesses can streamline their marketing efforts, reduce costs, and improve the ROI of their marketing campaigns.

Digital Transformation: Digital transformation refers to the integration of digital technologies into all areas of a business, including operations, customer service, marketing, and more. This can include using technologies such as artificial intelligence, machine learning, and big data analytics to improve decision-making and business outcomes. By embracing digital transformation, businesses can increase their agility, reduce costs, and scale more efficiently. For example, businesses can use big data analytics to gain insights into customer behavior and improve their marketing strategies.

In conclusion, technology, beyond AI, can help businesses scale more efficiently in various ways. By leveraging automation, cloud computing, project management tools, marketing automation, and digital transformation, businesses can increase efficiency, reduce costs, and improve productivity. To remain competitive in today's fast-paced business environment, it is essential that businesses embrace the use of technology to scale their operations.

CHAPTER 11: MANAGING AND ADAPTING TO CHANGE

No business can survive without adapting to changes in the market and industry. Whether it's a new competitor entering the market, a change in consumer preferences or a shift in technology, businesses need to be agile and flexible in order to survive and thrive. In this chapter, we'll discuss the importance of being adaptable and offer tips for managing change effectively.

One of the key factors in managing change effectively is to be aware of what's happening in the market and industry. This means keeping up with the latest trends, technologies, and consumer behavior. By doing this, businesses can identify opportunities for growth and innovation, and anticipate potential challenges.

Another important aspect of managing change effectively is to be proactive rather than reactive. Instead of waiting for change to happen, businesses should actively seek out opportunities for improvement and growth. This could involve investing in new technologies, exploring new markets or developing new products and services.

Automation is one technology that can help businesses scale more efficiently. By automating repetitive tasks such as data entry, invoicing and customer support, businesses can free up time and resources to focus on more strategic activities. Automation can also help improve accuracy and consistency, leading to better customer experiences and improved efficiency.

Cloud computing is another technology that can help businesses scale more efficiently. By using cloud-based applications and services, businesses can reduce their reliance on expensive hardware and infrastructure, and access data and applications from anywhere in the world. Cloud computing also offers scalability, which means businesses can easily increase or decrease their usage as needed.

Project management tools are another technology that can help businesses manage change effectively. By using tools such as Trello, Asana or Basecamp, businesses can track projects, assign tasks and collaborate with team members, no matter where they are located. This can help ensure that projects are completed on time and within budget and can also help businesses respond quickly to changes in project scope or requirements.

In addition to technology, there are other strategies that businesses can use to manage change effectively. For example, businesses can invest in ongoing training and development for their employees, to ensure that they have the skills and knowledge needed to adapt to changing circumstances. They can also develop a strong company culture that values innovation, creativity and continuous improvement.

managing change effectively is essential for businesses that want to scale and grow. By being aware of what's happening in the market and industry, being proactive, and using technologies such as automation, cloud computing and project management tools, businesses can improve efficiency, reduce costs and improve customer experiences.

Here is a list of companies that have had success in adapting to changes in the market and industry:

Netflix: The streaming giant started as a DVD-by-mail service, but has since adapted to the rise of online streaming, creating original content and partnering with studios to provide exclusive content.

Amazon: Originally an online bookstore, Amazon has grown to become the largest online retailer in the world. The company has expanded into areas like cloud computing, streaming services, and grocery delivery, among others.

Apple: The company began as a computer manufacturer, but has since expanded to include products like smartphones, tablets, and wearables. Apple also revolutionized the music industry with the creation of the iTunes Store and has become a major player in the streaming entertainment space with Apple TV+.

Microsoft: Originally focused on computer software, Microsoft has expanded into gaming, hardware, and cloud computing. The company has also successfully pivoted its business model multiple times, most notably with the transition from selling software to offering it as a subscription service.

Tesla: The electric car company disrupted the automotive industry with its innovative technology and sustainable focus. Tesla has also expanded into the energy sector with the creation of solar panels and battery storage.

Airbnb: The online platform disrupted the hospitality industry by allowing individuals to rent out their homes or apartments to travelers. The company has since expanded into other areas like experiences and luxury travel accommodations.

Uber: The ride-sharing company disrupted the traditional taxi industry by allowing anyone with a car to become a driver. Uber has since expanded into other areas like food delivery and electric bikes and scooters.

Salesforce: The software company disrupted the traditional model of selling software by offering it as a subscription service. Salesforce has also expanded into areas like marketing automation and customer relationship management.

Shopify: The e-commerce platform has helped small businesses compete with larger retailers by providing tools to create online stores and manage inventory, shipping, and payments. Shopify has also expanded into areas like payment processing and social media advertising.

Slack: The messaging app has disrupted traditional workplace communication by providing a platform for team collaboration and project management. Slack has also expanded into areas like video conferencing and virtual events.

In order for a business to succeed, it must be flexible and agile in the face of changes in the market and industry. This chapter stresses the importance of being adaptable and provides tips for managing change effectively. To manage change effectively, businesses must stay up-to-date with the latest trends, technologies, and consumer behavior, allowing them to anticipate potential challenges and identify opportunities for growth and innovation. Additionally, being proactive rather than reactive can help businesses seek out opportunities for improvement and growth. Technology such as automation, cloud computing, and project management tools can help businesses scale more efficiently, reduce costs, and improve customer experiences. Other strategies such as investing in ongoing training and development for employees and cultivating a strong company culture that values innovation, creativity, and continuous improvement can also help businesses manage change effectively. Overall, managing change effectively is essential for businesses that want to scale and grow, and staying adaptable is key to long-term success.

CHAPTER 12: EXPANDING YOUR BUSINESS GLOBALLY

Expanding your business globally can present several challenges and opportunities. On one hand, it can open new markets and revenue streams, while on the other hand, it requires significant resources and investment. In this chapter, we will explore the benefits and challenges of global expansion and offer strategies for success.

Benefits of Global Expansion

One of the primary benefits of global expansion is the potential for increased revenue and market share. By expanding into new markets, businesses can tap into new customer segments and access new sources of revenue. Additionally, global expansion can help businesses diversify their revenue streams, reducing their dependence on a single market or region.

Global expansion can also provide opportunities for cost savings and operational efficiencies. For example, businesses may be able to access lower-cost suppliers, take advantage of favorable exchange rates, and streamline their supply chains.

Finally, global expansion can enhance a company's reputation and brand recognition. By expanding into new markets, businesses can build brand awareness and reputation, and demonstrate their commitment to growth and innovation.

Challenges of Global Expansion

While there are many benefits to global expansion, there are also a number of challenges that businesses must consider. One of the biggest challenges is cultural differences. Every country has its own unique customs, traditions, and ways of doing business, and businesses must be able to adapt to these differences in order to succeed.

Another challenge is legal and regulatory compliance. Businesses must comply with a range of laws and regulations in each country they operate in, and failure to do so can result in significant legal and financial penalties.

Finally, there is the challenge of managing a global workforce. Businesses must be able to recruit, train, and manage employees in multiple countries, and must ensure that they comply with local labor laws and regulations.

Strategies for Success

Despite the challenges of global expansion, there are a number of strategies that businesses can use to succeed. Here are some key strategies to consider:

Conduct market research: Before expanding into a new market, businesses should conduct thorough market research to understand the local customs, preferences, and competition.

Develop a strong global strategy: Businesses should develop a comprehensive global strategy that takes into account cultural differences, legal and regulatory requirements, and operational considerations.

Build a local presence: Businesses should establish a local presence in each market they operate in, whether through partnerships, joint ventures, or subsidiaries.

Focus on talent acquisition and management: Hiring and retaining top talent is essential for success in any market, but particularly in global markets where cultural differences and local labor laws can create additional challenges.

Partner with local experts: Businesses can benefit from partnering with local experts, including consultants, advisors, and suppliers who have experience and knowledge of the local market.

Continuously evaluate and adjust: Global markets are constantly changing, and businesses must be able to adapt and adjust their strategies and operations to stay competitive.

Expanding your business globally can be a challenging but rewarding endeavor. By understanding the benefits and challenges of global expansion, and by adopting effective strategies for success, businesses can tap into new markets, increase revenue, and enhance their reputation and brand recognition.

One example of a company using AI to expand globally is Alibaba. Alibaba is a Chinese multinational conglomerate specializing in e-commerce, retail, Internet, and technology. The company's AI platform, Aliyun, uses natural language processing and machine learning algorithms to help businesses expand globally.

Aliyun offers a suite of tools designed to help businesses sell their products in new markets, including language translation, product listings, and customer service. The platform also provides real-time analytics and insights, allowing businesses to make data-driven decisions about where to focus their marketing efforts and expand their operations.

Another example of a company using AI to expand globally is Airbnb.

Airbnb is a peer-to-peer online marketplace that allows people to rent out their homes or apartments to travelers. The company uses AI to personalize the experience for each user, based on their preferences and past booking history.

Airbnb's AI-powered search algorithm takes into account a wide range of factors, including location, price, and amenities, to help users find the perfect place to stay. The company also uses AI to optimize pricing and manage inventory, ensuring that hosts are earning the maximum amount of revenue and that guests have access to the widest selection of properties.

Finally, there is Amazon, which is using AI to expand globally in a variety of ways. For example, the company's AI-powered language translation service, Amazon Translate, allows businesses to communicate with customers in multiple languages, without the need for human translators.

Amazon is also using AI to improve its logistics and supply chain management. The company's autonomous delivery drones use machine learning algorithms to navigate complex environments and avoid obstacles, making it possible to deliver packages to remote or hard-to-reach locations. There are many real-world examples of companies using AI to expand globally. By leveraging the power of machine learning and natural language processing, these companies are able to personalize the customer experience, optimize pricing and inventory, and communicate with customers in multiple languages. As AI technology continues to advance, we can expect to see even more companies using these tools to grow their businesses and expand into new markets.

Global expansion offers a range of benefits for businesses today. First and foremost, expanding globally can provide access to new markets and customer segments, which can result in increased revenue and market share. This is particularly important for businesses that operate in mature markets, where growth may be limited.

In addition, global expansion can help businesses diversify their revenue streams and reduce their dependence on a single market or region. This can be particularly valuable during times of economic uncertainty or disruption, as businesses with a diverse customer base are often better able to weather downturns.

Global expansion can also provide opportunities for cost savings and operational efficiencies. For example, businesses may be able to access lower-cost suppliers, take advantage of favorable exchange rates, and streamline their supply chains. This can result in lower costs and improved profit margins.

Finally, global expansion can enhance a company's reputation and brand recognition. By expanding into new markets, businesses can build brand awareness and reputation, and demonstrate their commitment to growth and innovation. This can help attract new customers and talent and can also improve a company's bargaining power with suppliers and partners.

While global expansion can be challenging, the potential benefits are significant. By carefully considering the challenges and opportunities of global expansion, and by adopting effective strategies for success, businesses can successfully expand into new markets and realize the benefits of global growth.

CHAPTER 13: NAVIGATING LEGAL AND REGULATORY COMPLIANCE

As a business grows, it becomes subject to a more complex legal and regulatory landscape. To ensure success, business owners need to be aware of the key compliance issues they face and stay on top of the legal requirements they must meet. This chapter will provide an overview of some of the most important compliance issues that businesses face and offer tips for staying compliant.

Business Entity Formation

When starting a business, owners must decide on the type of entity to form. The most common types of business entities include sole proprietorships, partnerships, limited liability companies (LLCs), and corporations. Each entity type has its own legal and tax implications, so it is important to choose the right entity for your business.

For example, an LLC provides limited liability protection for owners and is taxed like a partnership, while a corporation is a separate legal entity that can issue stock and has its own tax rules. By choosing the right entity type, business owners can ensure they are meeting legal and tax requirements and protecting themselves from personal liability.

Employment Laws

Employment laws can be complex and vary by state and country. Businesses must comply with regulations governing minimum wage, overtime pay, discrimination, harassment, and safety in the workplace, among other things.

To stay compliant, business owners should consult with an employment lawyer to understand their obligations and create policies and procedures to ensure compliance. They should also provide regular training for employees to prevent violations of employment laws.

Taxation

Businesses are subject to various taxes, including income tax, payroll tax, sales tax, and property tax. To ensure compliance with tax laws, businesses must keep accurate records and file tax returns on time.

It is important for business owners to consult with a tax professional to understand their tax obligations and take advantage of any available deductions or credits. They should also develop a system for record-keeping and implement processes to ensure timely filing and payment of taxes.

Data Privacy and Security

As businesses collect and store more data, they become subject to increasingly stringent data privacy and security regulations. Businesses must protect sensitive information such as customer data and employee records from theft or unauthorized access.

To stay compliant, businesses should implement data privacy and security policies and procedures, and regularly review and update them to ensure they are keeping up with changing regulations. They should also provide regular training for employees on how to protect sensitive information.

Environmental Regulations

Businesses may also be subject to environmental regulations governing waste disposal, emissions, and other environmental impacts. These regulations can be complex and vary by industry and location.

To ensure compliance with environmental regulations, businesses should consult with an environmental lawyer and develop policies and procedures to minimize their environmental impact. They should also track their environmental performance and implement measures to reduce their impact over time.

Intellectual Property

Businesses must also protect their intellectual property, including trademarks, copyrights, and patents. Failure to do so can result in loss of revenue and damage to the company's reputation.

To ensure protection of their intellectual property, businesses should consult with an intellectual property lawyer and register their trademarks, copyrights, and patents. They should also monitor for infringements and take legal action when necessary.

Compliance is an essential aspect of running a successful business. By understanding the key compliance issues they face and taking steps to ensure compliance, business owners can protect themselves from legal and financial risks and ensure long-term success. Business owners should consult with legal and tax professionals to stay on top of changing regulations and develop policies and procedures to ensure compliance with applicable laws and regulations.

CHAPTER 14: BUILDING A SOCIALLY RESPONSIBLE BUSINESS

As consumers become increasingly aware of social and environmental issues, many businesses are recognizing the importance of being socially responsible. In addition to helping to make the world a better place, social responsibility can also be good for business, as it can help to attract customers, employees, and investors who share similar values. In this chapter, we will discuss the importance of social responsibility and offer strategies for building a business that makes a positive impact on the world.

Why Social Responsibility Matters

Social responsibility refers to the idea that businesses have a responsibility to act in the best interests of society and the environment, as well as their shareholders. There are a number of reasons why social responsibility is important:

Reputation and brand image: Social responsibility can enhance a company's reputation and brand image, as consumers are increasingly looking for companies that share their values and are committed to making a positive impact on the world.

Employee engagement and retention: Employees are more likely to be engaged and motivated if they feel that their work is making a positive difference in the world. In addition, socially responsible companies are more likely to attract and retain top talent.

Risk management: Socially responsible companies are better able to manage risks associated with environmental and social issues, such as climate change and labor practices, which can have a significant impact on a company's bottom line.

Access to capital: Investors are increasingly looking for socially responsible companies to invest in, and companies that are committed to social responsibility may have access to a wider range of capital sources.

Here are some strategies for building a socially responsible business:

Develop a mission and values statement: A mission and values statement can help to guide a company's decision-making and ensure that it is aligned with its social and environmental goals. Conduct a social and environmental impact assessment: A social and environmental impact assessment can help to identify the social and environmental risks and opportunities associated with a company's operations.

Implement responsible sourcing practices: Responsible sourcing practices can help to ensure that a company's supply chain is free from forced labor, child labor, and other unethical practices. Reduce environmental impact: Companies can reduce their environmental impact by implementing sustainable practices, such as reducing waste and energy consumption, and using renewable energy sources.

Support the local community: Companies can support the local community by partnering with local organizations and charities, volunteering, and donating a portion of their profits to social causes.

Engage stakeholders: Companies can engage stakeholders, including customers, employees, and investors, in their social and environmental efforts, which can help to build support for their initiatives and strengthen their reputation.

Measure and report on social and environmental performance: Measuring and reporting on social and environmental performance can help to demonstrate a company's commitment to social responsibility and provide transparency to stakeholders.

Building a socially responsible business can be a challenging but rewarding endeavor. By implementing strategies to reduce social and environmental risks and maximize social and environmental opportunities, companies can enhance their reputation, attract and retain top talent, manage risks, and access a wider range of capital sources. By embracing social responsibility, companies can not only make a positive impact on the world but also build a stronger and more sustainable business.

CHAPTER 15: UNSTOPPABLE!

Artificial intelligence (AI) has the potential to revolutionize the way businesses generate ideas and innovate. In this chapter, we will explore how AI can be used to help businesses generate new and innovative ideas, and offer strategies for incorporating AI into the innovation process.

The Importance of Innovation

Innovation is crucial for businesses to remain competitive and relevant in today's fast-paced and ever-changing market. The ability to generate new and unique ideas is what sets successful businesses apart from their competitors. Innovation can help businesses increase revenue, reduce costs, improve efficiency, and create new products and services that meet the evolving needs of customers.

The Role of AI in Innovation

AI can play a significant role in the innovation process by assisting businesses in generating new and innovative ideas. AI can analyze data, identify patterns, and make predictions based on past behaviors and trends, helping businesses make more informed decisions about product development, market research, and customer engagement.

One of the key benefits of AI in innovation is its ability to analyze vast amounts of data quickly and accurately. This can help businesses identify patterns and trends that might otherwise go unnoticed, allowing them to make more informed decisions about product development and marketing strategies.

AI can also help businesses identify gaps in the market and new opportunities for growth. By analyzing customer behavior and preferences, AI can help businesses identify emerging trends and changing consumer needs, enabling them to develop new products and services that meet these needs.

In addition, AI can help businesses improve the efficiency and effectiveness of their innovation process by automating certain tasks and freeing up human resources for more creative and strategic work. For example, AI can assist with market research, product testing, and idea generation, allowing businesses to focus on bringing their most innovative ideas to fruition.

Here are some strategies that businesses can use to incorporate AI into their innovation process: Identify areas where AI can add value: The first step in incorporating AI into the innovation process is to identify areas where it can add the most value. This might include market research, customer engagement, product development, or idea generation.

Collect and analyze data: Once you have identified the areas where AI can add value, the next step is to collect and analyze relevant data. This might include customer data, sales data, or industry trends.

Use AI to analyze data and identify patterns: Once you have collected data, you can use AI to analyze it and identify patterns and trends. This can help you make more informed decisions about product development, marketing strategies, and customer engagement.

Collaborate with AI: AI can be used to collaborate with humans in the innovation process. For example, businesses can use AI-powered chatbots to gather customer feedback and input or use AI to assist with brainstorming and idea generation.

Experiment and iterate: Finally, it's important to experiment and iterate with AI in the innovation process. Try new approaches, test different strategies, and measure the results to identify what works best for your business.

AI has the potential to revolutionize the way businesses generate ideas and innovate. By incorporating AI into the innovation process, businesses can analyze data, identify trends, and make more informed decisions about product development, marketing strategies, and customer engagement. By following the strategies outlined in this chapter, businesses can leverage AI to create new and innovative products and services that meet the changing needs of customers and stay ahead of the competition.

By incorporating AI into the innovation process, businesses can create an "unstoppable" business that is constantly evolving and adapting to changing market conditions. By analyzing vast amounts of data quickly and accurately, AI can help businesses stay ahead of emerging trends and identify new opportunities for growth.

AI can help businesses streamline their innovation process and reduce costs by automating certain tasks and freeing up human resources for more creative and strategic work. This can lead to a more efficient and effective innovation process, allowing businesses to bring their most innovative ideas to market faster.

The integration of AI into the innovation process can help businesses create new and unique ideas, improve efficiency and effectiveness, and stay ahead of the competition in a rapidly evolving market. By embracing AI, businesses can unlock the full potential of innovation and create an "unstoppable" business that is poised for long-term success.

CHAPTER 16: INTEGRATING AI INTO YOUR BUSINESS OPERATIONS

Artificial intelligence (AI) has the potential to revolutionize the way businesses operate. By automating processes, analyzing data, and making predictions, AI can help companies increase efficiency, reduce costs, and improve productivity. In this chapter, we will explore how businesses can incorporate AI and automation technologies into their daily operations to achieve these benefits.

The Benefits of AI Integration
Integrating AI into business operations can bring many benefits, such as:

Improved Efficiency: AI can automate routine and repetitive tasks, freeing up employees to focus on higher-level tasks that require creativity and critical thinking. This can result in increased productivity and faster turnaround times.

Enhanced Decision-Making: AI can analyze large amounts of data quickly and accurately, providing businesses with valuable insights that can inform strategic decision-making.

Cost Reduction: By automating tasks and processes, businesses can reduce the need for manual labor, leading to cost savings and improved profitability.

Increased Customer Satisfaction: AI-powered tools, such as chatbots and virtual assistants, can provide 24/7 customer support, improving the customer experience and increasing satisfaction.

Implementing AI into Your Operations
To successfully integrate AI into your business operations, you will need to take the following steps:

Identify Areas for AI Implementation: Identify areas within your business where AI could be applied, such as customer service, supply chain management, or inventory management.

Determine Data Needs: Determine the types of data that will be required to support AI implementation, such as customer data or sales data.

Choose an AI Solution: Select an AI solution that meets your business needs and integrates with your existing systems. This may involve building your own AI solution, purchasing a commercial solution, or outsourcing to a third-party vendor.

Train Employees: Ensure that employees receive training on how to use AI tools and understand their benefits.

Monitor and Evaluate: Continuously monitor the performance of your AI implementation and evaluate its effectiveness. Use data to refine your implementation over time and make necessary adjustments.

Best Practices for AI Integration
To maximize the benefits of AI integration, businesses should follow these best practices:

Start Small: Begin with a pilot project to test the effectiveness of AI implementation before scaling it up.

Focus on the End User: When designing AI-powered tools, consider the needs and preferences of end-users to ensure the best possible user experience.

Maintain Transparency: Be transparent about the use of AI within your business operations, both internally and externally, to build trust with employees and customers.

Ensure Security: Ensure that your AI implementation is secure and complies with relevant data protection and privacy regulations.

Emphasize Human Oversight: AI should never replace human decision-making entirely. Ensure that human oversight is maintained throughout the

AI implementation process to ensure ethical decision-making.

Integrating AI into business operations has the potential to bring significant benefits to companies of all sizes. By automating routine tasks, analyzing data, and making predictions, AI can help businesses increase efficiency, reduce costs, and improve productivity. To successfully integrate AI, businesses should start small, focus on end-users, maintain transparency, ensure security, and emphasize human oversight. With careful planning and execution, AI can become an invaluable tool for businesses looking to stay competitive in a rapidly changing landscape.

CHAPTER 17: ETHICAL CONSIDERATIONS FOR AI IN BUSINESS

Artificial Intelligence (AI) is increasingly being integrated into various industries and business operations worldwide. While AI brings several benefits, including increased efficiency, accuracy, and productivity, there are also ethical concerns that need to be addressed. In this chapter, we will explore some of the ethical considerations for AI in business, including bias, privacy concerns, and how companies can address these issues.

Bias:

One of the most significant ethical considerations for AI in business is the issue of bias. Bias can occur when the algorithms that power AI are trained on biased data or when the developers themselves hold biases. For instance, facial recognition technology has been found to be less accurate for people with darker skin tones, as the algorithms were often trained on datasets dominated by lighter-skinned individuals. This can have serious consequences, such as perpetuating racial profiling and discrimination.

To address the issue of bias, companies must ensure that their AI systems are trained on diverse datasets and are regularly audited for biases. Developers must also take care to examine their own biases and ensure that they do not impact the development of the AI system.

Privacy Concerns:

Another ethical consideration for AI in business is privacy concerns. As AI collects and processes vast amounts of data, there is a risk that this data can be used to invade people's privacy. For instance, AI-powered surveillance systems can be used to track people's movements and behaviors, raising concerns about civil liberties and surveillance. Companies must ensure that they are transparent about the data they collect and how it is used. They must also ensure that they comply with data privacy laws and regulations, such as the General Data Protection Regulation (GDPR).

Transparency:

Transparency is another important ethical consideration for AI in business. As AI systems become more complex, it can be challenging to understand how they work and how they make decisions. This lack of transparency can have serious consequences, such as perpetuating discrimination or making it difficult to hold companies accountable for their actions. Companies must ensure that their AI systems are transparent, and that they can explain how decisions are made. This can be achieved through the use of interpretable models or by providing detailed documentation of the algorithms used.

Human Oversight:

Finally, human oversight is an essential ethical consideration for AI in business. While AI can automate many tasks, there are some tasks that should not be left entirely to machines. For instance, AI systems that make decisions that impact people's lives, such as hiring decisions, should be subject to human oversight. Companies must ensure that humans are involved in the development and implementation of AI systems, and that they have the power to override decisions made by the AI system.

AI has enormous potential to transform business operations and bring significant benefits. However, it is essential to address the ethical considerations that arise from using AI in business. Companies must ensure that their AI systems are free from bias, protect people's privacy, are transparent, and subject to human oversight. By doing so, companies can ensure that they are using AI in a responsible and ethical manner.

CHAPTER 18: THE FUTURE OF AI IN BUSINESS

Artificial Intelligence (AI) has been transforming the business landscape for several years, but it is clear that we are only at the beginning of the potential of AI in business. In this chapter, we will explore the potential future applications of AI in business, including predictive analytics, autonomous decision-making, and other emerging trends.

Predictive Analytics:

One of the most promising applications of AI in business is predictive analytics. Predictive analytics uses AI algorithms to analyze large datasets to predict future outcomes. For example, in finance, predictive analytics can be used to predict market trends, while in retail, it can be used to predict customer behavior. Predictive analytics can also be used in healthcare to predict disease outbreaks or to identify patients at risk of developing certain conditions.

As AI becomes more advanced, the accuracy of predictive analytics is likely to increase, leading to more informed decision-making and better outcomes for businesses.

Autonomous Decision-Making:

Another potential application of AI in business is autonomous decision-making. Autonomous decision-making involves AI systems making decisions without human intervention. For instance, in manufacturing, AI-powered robots can make decisions about which parts to assemble next, or in logistics, AI can make decisions about the most efficient delivery routes.

While the idea of autonomous decision-making can be intimidating for some, it has the potential to increase efficiency and productivity significantly. However, companies must ensure that their AI systems are transparent and that they can explain how decisions are made to maintain trust and accountability.

Customer Experience:

AI has already transformed the customer experience in many industries, and it is likely to continue to do so in the future. For instance, chatbots and virtual assistants are already being used in customer service to provide faster and more personalized support.

In the future, AI is likely to enable even more personalized customer experiences, with AI systems analyzing vast amounts of data to predict customer preferences and provide personalized recommendations. This could revolutionize the way businesses interact with their customers, providing them with an even more seamless and enjoyable experience.

Other Emerging Trends:

There are also several other emerging trends in the field of AI that are likely to have a significant impact on business. For instance, explainable AI is becoming increasingly important, as companies seek to understand how their AI systems make decisions. Edge computing, which involves processing data on devices themselves rather than in the cloud, is also becoming more important, as it allows AI systems to operate in real-time.

The future of AI in business is bright, with enormous potential to transform the way businesses operate and interact with their customers. As AI becomes more advanced, we can expect to see more accurate predictive analytics, more autonomous decision-making, and more personalized customer experiences. However, it is essential that companies continue to address the ethical considerations surrounding the use of AI, such as transparency and accountability. By doing so, we can ensure that AI is used in a responsible and ethical manner, leading to positive outcomes for businesses and society as a whole.

CHAPTER 19: AI AND CYBERSECURITY

As businesses become increasingly reliant on technology, cybersecurity is becoming an increasingly pressing concern. The threat of cyber-attacks is higher than ever before, and companies must take measures to protect themselves from these threats. One promising technology that can help companies enhance their cybersecurity measures is Artificial Intelligence (AI). In this chapter, we will explore the ways in which AI can be used to enhance cybersecurity measures and protect businesses from cyber threats.

Threat Detection and Response:

One of the most important applications of AI in cybersecurity is threat detection and response. AI-powered systems can analyze vast amounts of data in real-time, identifying potential threats and anomalies that may indicate an attack. This can help companies to respond quickly to potential threats, preventing damage and minimizing downtime.

AI can also be used to automate threat response, taking action to prevent or mitigate the effects of an attack without human intervention. For example, an AI-powered system can isolate a compromised machine from the network, preventing the spread of malware.

Fraud Prevention:

AI can also be used to prevent fraud in business operations. AI algorithms can detect patterns and anomalies in financial transactions, identifying potentially fraudulent activity. This can help businesses to prevent fraud before it occurs, saving them time and money.

In addition, AI-powered fraud prevention systems can learn from past fraud attempts, becoming more effective over time. This means that they can adapt to new types of fraud, staying ahead of the curve and protecting businesses from new threats.

Vulnerability Management:

Another important application of AI in cybersecurity is vulnerability management. AI-powered systems can identify vulnerabilities in a company's systems and applications, alerting the appropriate personnel so that they can be patched. This can help companies to stay ahead of potential attacks, closing vulnerabilities before they can be exploited.

AI can also help to prioritize vulnerabilities, identifying those that are most critical and need to be patched first. This can help companies to allocate their resources more effectively, focusing on the most critical vulnerabilities first.

AI has enormous potential to enhance cybersecurity measures and protect businesses from cyber threats. From threat detection and response to fraud prevention and vulnerability management, AI-powered systems can provide businesses with the tools they need to stay ahead of potential attacks. However, it is essential that companies address the ethical considerations surrounding the use of AI in cybersecurity, such as transparency and accountability. By doing so, we can ensure that AI is used in a responsible and ethical manner, leading to positive outcomes for businesses and society as a whole.

CONCLUSION:

Throughout this book, we discussed the important role of AI in achieving business success. We explored various ways that AI can be used to help businesses identify their target audience, analyze customer data, create a strong brand, recruit top talent, manage finances, optimize product development, execute successful marketing campaigns, and identify growth opportunities.

We provided real examples of successful businesses that have implemented AI to improve various aspects of their operations, such as Amazon, Spotify, and Netflix. Additionally, we emphasized the importance of developing a clear business mission and goals, collecting, and analyzing customer data, building a strong team, and focusing on high-quality products and services.

We discussed how AI can help businesses overcome various challenges associated with scaling, such as identifying growth opportunities and optimizing resources. Ultimately, businesses that successfully implement AI in their operations can gain a competitive edge in today's rapidly evolving marketplace.

As you've read through the various topics and strategies discussed in this book, we hope you've gained valuable insights and inspiration for building and growing your own business. Remember, while AI can be a powerful tool, it's ultimately up to you to apply these concepts and techniques in a way that's relevant and effective for your unique situation. We encourage you to take what you've learned and start experimenting and implementing new strategies in your business today. With dedication and hard work, you too can achieve the kind of success that the companies mentioned in this content have experienced. Best of luck on your journey!

Remember, implementing AI in your business requires a thoughtful and strategic approach. It's important to stay informed and continue learning as new developments in the field emerge. Good luck on your journey towards creating an unstoppable business!

DISCLAIMER:

Disclaimer: The information provided in this book is for general informational and educational purposes only. It is not intended to provide legal, financial, or other professional advice. The publisher of this content makes no representations or warranties of any kind, express or implied, about the completeness, accuracy, reliability, suitability, or availability with respect to the information, products, services, or related graphics contained in this chat for any purpose. Any reliance you place on such information is therefore strictly at your own risk. In no event will the publisher be liable for any loss or damage including without limitation, indirect or consequential loss or damage, or any loss or damage whatsoever arising from loss of data or profits arising out of, or in connection with, the use of this information.

ALL ILLUSTRATIONS IN THIS BOOK WERE
GENERATED USING AI.

A BIZZAR FABLE

Once upon a time, in a distant galaxy far, far away, there existed a planet called Bizzar, inhabited by intelligent beings known as Bizarians. They were known throughout the universe for their mastery in the art of building and running businesses.

One day, the Bizarians received a message from an alien civilization. The message contained the secrets of a powerful tool called AI, which had the ability to transform businesses into unstoppable forces. The Bizarians were excited to learn more about this tool and its potential to enhance their business skills.

They set out to discover more about AI, studying and experimenting with its capabilities to unlock its full potential. With the help of AI, they were able to identify and analyze their target market and optimize their products and services. They were also able to recruit the best talent and manage their finances more efficiently.

AI helped them to create a strong and memorable brand that resonated with their customers. By collecting and analyzing customer data, they were able to develop personalized marketing campaigns that generated a high level of engagement and loyalty.

As the Bizarians continued to implement AI into their business practices, they began to experience tremendous growth and success. They were able to scale their businesses to unprecedented levels, reaching new heights of success that they had never imagined possible.

The Bizarians realized that AI was truly a powerful tool that could transform any business into an unstoppable force. They shared their knowledge and expertise with other planets, spreading the word about the power of AI and its ability to revolutionize the business world.

And so, the Bizarians became known throughout the universe for their ability to build and run businesses that were unstoppable, and they lived happily ever after.

ABOUT THE AUTHOR

Torrey Hash is an entrepreneur and business leader, and this is his first book. As the founder of Hashtagz LLC, an online digital media marketing company with industry interests in advertising, graphic design, and crypto, he has been at the forefront of digital innovation and disruption. Torrey is a trailblazer in the use of AI in business and has successfully implemented AI strategies and solutions that have improved efficiency, enhanced customer experiences, and driven innovation. Through his company, Torrey helps businesses leverage AI to achieve long-term success in today's competitive economy. As an emerging thought leader in the field of AI and business strategy, Torrey is passionate about sharing his knowledge and expertise with others.